YOUR DESTINY IS
IN YOUR HANDS
The Winning Strategy

TESSY L. AGUZIE PH.D

WESTBOW
P R E S S®
A DIVISION OF THOMAS NELSON
& ZONDERVAN

Scripture taken from the King James Version of the Bible.

The information, ideas, and suggestions in this book are not intended as a substitute for professional advice. Before following any suggestions contained in this book, you should consult your personal physician or mental health professional. Neither the author nor the publisher shall be liable or responsible for any loss or damage allegedly arising as a consequence of your use or application of any information or suggestions in this book.

WestBow Press books may be ordered through booksellers or by contacting:

WestBow Press
A Division of Thomas Nelson & Zondervan
1663 Liberty Drive
Bloomington, IN 47403
www.westbowpress.com
1 (866) 928-1240

Because of the dynamic nature of the Internet, any web addresses or links contained in this book may have changed since publication and may no longer be valid. The views expressed in this work are solely those of the author and do not necessarily reflect the views of the publisher, and the publisher hereby disclaims any responsibility for them.

Any people depicted in stock imagery provided by Thinkstock are models, and such images are being used for illustrative purposes only. Certain stock imagery © Thinkstock.

ISBN: 978-1-5127-9459-5 (sc)
ISBN: 978-1-5127-9495-3 (hc)
ISBN: 978-1-5127-9460-1 (e)

Library of Congress Control Number: 2017910949

Print information available on the last page.

WestBow Press rev. date: 07/18/2017

Contents

Dedication

This book is dedicated to God almighty, and to the four walls of my life. To my love Christopher Agbanyim, to my entire family who has always been my inspirations, to my friends and to the entire members of Rescue the Sinners Ministry.

Acknowledgement

I want to appreciate the great men and women of God that has contributed in my life. Apostle Emmanuel Maiyaki, prophetess Doris Johnson and to my spiritual father Rev. Chinekeokwu RKC and his lovely wife Unique for their support in making this dream a reality.

Introduction

Strategic planning is often the best practice both in business and every other aspect of life. The level to which you understand a situation gives you added advantage over others. Men who often strategize before unleashing do not always miss their targets. This means that your level of understanding of a particular situation will create an opportunity for you to aim well for success. Most of life challenges are common, several people have experienced what you are facing right now, and it will be easy for you to understand how those people won or lost those challenges. People often say experience is the best teacher, but I said you don't often need the experience before you learn rather you can learn from other people's experiences. The question is, why is it that individuals with great destiny always suffer at the beginning of their life? The answer is detailed in this book.

First, we do not wrestle against flesh and blood but principalities, powers and rulers of darkness in high places. 2nd Cor. 10:4 (NLT)

Remember the scripture said in high places, not low places. This means that when you are trying to rise from one level in life to another, you have the territorial stronghold in that level to fight with. In other words, before you move from level one to two or better still primary one to two, you have to write and pass exams. If you fail these exams, you will have to rewrite them until you pass. Remember your adversary the devil has been in the picture long before you came. The same devil in the Garden of Eden, during the time of Job and the time of Jesus, is still in the picture. This same devil has seen a lot of people that act and behave like you. Sometimes he can predict some of the things you can do unless you operate in the power of the Holy Ghost who is ahead of Satan in the game of life. Therefore, understanding the strategic steps from great people of the past and to understand how you can avoid being your stumbling block will help you to fight the right way and win in life. All you require to be successful is already in you. So quit waiting for God to change your life but through prayer and conscious strategic actions, you will change your life for better. The mechanism is in your mind. Stop looking for a solution to this tragic life outside you rather look inside. Use your intuition than focusing on the outside stimulus because you have been equipped by God. The principle you will learn from this book will guide you to understand the human ability given by God Almighty. This strategic way of operation will help you in the affairs of life when you learn to pray and declare strategically to overpower the wicked enemies in high places.

Chapter One

SPIRIT REALM

First I want you to understand that there is something called the spirit realm. This realm is as real as my right hand. Whether you believe it or not, this domain controls the physical realm. This means that before anything happens in the physical, it has already taken place in the spiritual and not long, it will manifest in the physical. The battles of life are being fought and win or lose in the spiritual realm. A man is a spirit living in a body (Earth suite) as soon as this earth suit is removed; man seizes to function as human but as a spirit. Every change you want to make in your life can be done now that you still have your earth suit. In other words, once this suite is removed the history is already made and not about to be made. Man functions in three-dimensional ways the **spirit, the soul, and the body.** We are three-dimensional being, operating through **our conscious, subconscious and super-conscious mind.** These three controls your entire life.

Invisible structure of your mind

Your subconscious mind is the powerhouse that helps you to create your world. The beauty or the ugliness of your life is coiled around this truth. And the more you understand how to frame your world to advance positively, the more successful you will become. Remember this success am talking about is not just in the area of money but in every aspect of your life. So there is no need to limit this understanding to the poor because you can be rich and be sickly or you can be healthy and poor. With your conscious mind, you make choices which are played out in your subconscious mind, and it is stored in your super conscious. Your five physical senses are the agents that channel all your choices to your subconscious through your conscious mind.

Clearly, your five senses is often a pathway that

channel all your experiences. This is done through touch (skin), what you smell (nose), what you taste (tongue), your ear (hear) and what you see (eyes) into your heart and out of the abundant of the heart, your mouth speaks. Since you are talking it means that we create our world with our word. Therefore, whatever is this experiences that have been communicated to your heart through these physical senses and have been declared through our word becomes our physical reality. Because it was registered by the subconscious mind as you think about it and you vocalize (speak) it. The duty of the subconscious mind is to bring to you all the opportunities required to accomplish that which was stored in it.

There is no room for un-seriousness

The interesting part is that your Subconscious mind does not know when you are serious or not, when you are joking or when you are just kidding. For those who play American way "am just kidding." Whatever you speak or think is what your subconscious mind believed that you want and it will begin to attract everything to produce the desired result which you wired into it. When you listen to music, whatever you sing through the music, your subconscious mind believed that you are speaking to him. So when you say I will die without you in a sweet romantic song, the subconscious mind already taking into account who or what you are referring to. Remember this is not a natural human that you can relate to and convince the opposite at that moment. This mind is you, and it understands you more than you can narrate yourself. For example, if the song is referring to this object or the precious person you have in your mind which could be your husband, wife, boyfriend, girlfriend, children, business, car or a house. It doesn't matter what form or shape that is. As soon as you sing "I will die without you," your conscious mind has taken note of that. What happens is that as soon as the person or the object left, your subconscious mind will begin to communicate to other parts of your body that your choice is to die in the absence of that individual. Don't misunderstand me; you may not fall and die instantly but the subconscious mind will begin to attract those things that will bring to pass this desired goal that you have spoken. May be it is already too many years back. This may result in a sickness, disease or even poverty that can cause your death. The same applies to the good songs you sang. For example when you sing favor is my name, and I don't worry about tomorrow. The same reaction takes place. Your subconscious also will continue to attract everything consistent with support and devoid of concern. This is science which is also consistent with the word of God. Have you not read the scriptures?

"As you have spoken to my hearing so will I do to you." (NUM, 14 VS 28 KJV)

Sometimes people argue that this Bible quotation is what we say only in the presence of God or maybe in the church or just when we pray. Have you forgotten that God is Omnipresence this means that he is everywhere even in your worst case scenario, He is there watching you?

What you think often, you create into existence.

All your thoughts, choices, words, feelings,

believe system, imaginations and what you listen to is often stored in your mind which turns out to become a reality. Therefore, as a man thinks in his heart so is he (PROV.23 VS 7 KJV). Your subconscious mind is like a computer, it only plays back whatever you stored on it. Only 2% of what you do is consciously controlled, but your subconscious mind controls 98%. Paramount question, can you regulate your temperature to be warm or cold internally? Can you pump your blood; do you control your arteries and veins to transport the right amount of fluid to your system? If not what does all of these? Listen, you are consciously in control of about 2-3% of your life, the rest is subconsciously controlled, but you are responsible for wiring in what the subconscious will work with. You indirectly control your subconscious mind. Your continuous thought often comes to reality, and your thinking controls your brain through the actions of your subconscious mind. This is why you should always renew your mind. Your five senses are your USB drive that connects information from the world into your mind. Whatever beliefs you hold in your subconscious mind, will shape your reality. This means

- If you believe you are a failure, yes you are
- If you feel you are poor, yes you are
- If you believe you are disadvantaged, yes you are
- If you believe you are a success, yes you are
- If you believe you are victorious, yes you are
- If you believe you will make it yes you will
- If you believe that you are a millionaire, yes you are.

Remember God never made a failure, the Bible said that all that God created is beautiful (GEN. 1 VS 31). This means that there is a seed of greatness inside you. It also means that you are well packaged before you came. It also means that you are well packaged for every challenge of life. All you need to be successful is already deposited inside of you. Therefore, how fruitful and victorious you will ever attain in this life depends on your ability to use the endowment bestowed by God inside you and, God has nothing to do about it. This only means that you quit blaming God for your condition and blame yourself for your ignorance of who you are. The Bible said I had given you choices, life, and death and you should choose right. The Bible also gave you a clue to choose right so that you and your generation will be saved. After this instruction whatever choices you make is not the doing of God but yours. It is often said after rain, comes the sun. This means that every choice has the follow-up consequences.

You cannot grow externally
until you grow internally

Make a decision to choose right

When you choose good, you will live well, but if you choose wrong, you will live poorly. So where are you right now? What choices have you been making? As I mentioned earlier, there is something called the spirit realm. In this field, a human being does not function with their earth suite but only in spirit. Whatever choice one makes has spiritual implications and these consequences whether good or bad has been done to transcend to your fourth generation. Evidently, in the scripture, Abraham lied and deceived due to fear of losing his wife and his life (GEN. 20 VS 2 KJV). Sarah lied probably because she heard about having a baby at age 90 which she thinks was impossible (GEN. 18 VS 12 KJV). Despite how right Abraham was, that lies transcend to his generation, apart from his grandson deceiving his father Jacob to obtain the blessing (GEN. 27 VS 1 KJV), Jacob was also lied to and deceived by his father-in-law Leban according to the scriptures in (Genesis 29:23-25 KJV). This is why it is vital for you as an individual to do the right thing so that you will save your children, even up to the fourth generation from the ripple effects.

So through your conscious mind, you make choices which are played out in your subconscious mind, and it is stored in your super conscious. All begins with your choice. Since your conscious mind never sleeps even when you are sleeping rather it continues to attract all that you have stored in it both the good the bad and the ugly. The pictures you consistently creates in your mind through your word and meditation often play back to your mind and since its your personal choice, your mind will begin to attract such things. What the enemy does is to manipulate you to interfere with your dreams giving you a negative picture which is held by your subconscious mind that will attract those negative things into your life. That is why he is called a deceiver.

When you begin to fear and shake
because of the devil, you will attract
him the more. (Rev .Dr P. Enenche)

Everything about the devil is a copy, I mean fake, falsehood."His sole purpose is to steal, kill and destroy" Note John 10:10 (NLT)

He does not have power anymore; Jesus has taken power from him. All he does is to use your personal power to kill you. He uses human being to destroy others by lying to them and painting pictures that look like the original, but it is all his lying strategies. However, when you understand the winning strategies already deposited inside of you by God Almighty, then you will make a conscious decision to be ahead of the enemy in all his tactics, you are always a winner in Christ Jesus.

Chapter Two

ALL THOUGHTS ARE CREATIVE

We are made in the image of God with the ability of God to be creative. Sadly people do not understand the mechanism of this creativity while others have been miss informed. Understanding the mechanism of your thoughts that is often played out in your word is a vital way to understanding the affairs of life since all thoughts are creative, it is essential to check what you concentrate your mind on. This thought creates your emotions and your emotions often define your personality. The chemical reactions that are generated in the brain through our experiences have the ability to shape your reality when it is nurtured consistently through the mood. This emotion becomes your personality. Neuroscience defined the mind as the brain in action or brain at work and emotion is energy in motion. Your personal reality is created by your character which includes how you feel and how you think. Any emotion you memorize is energy, and that connect to attract all the circumstances that are consistent with the feeling. If this emotion is linked from negative or positive past, the person creates a pattern of such experiences, and they see such experiences re-occurring over again. This is why so many people are stuck in a bad relationship because they continue to transfer their experiences of the past into their current relationship. At the end of the day, the same pattern of experience will re-occur but may be through another format.

"The quality of a person's life is determined by the amount of his thought and the limit of thought determines the limit of life".

Ask, and you shall receive (MATTHEW, 7 VS 7)

Life will give what you ask of it. That is why the Bible said asks and it shall be given to you. Jesus said those that asked received. This means that what you ask in life is what life will bring to you. I am not talking about complaining, grumbling or whining like a child. It is about specificity. Asking wisely is a key to receiving what you want from life because life will pay any price you ask of it. So many people do not know what they want. They only follow the direction life takes them, but life is much better than this. You were created in the image of God, and all the ability of God is in a Man. If we are like God, then we need to have a good taste with all capacity to create all that we want. The Bible said that the heavenly road was made with gold (REV. 21 VS 21 KJV). For us human, we put on Gold on our neck and hands, but God used Gold on the street. That is to tell you that God is classy and we have the same ability to create what we want. Because he is a loving God he wants us to love him genuinely with our heart, and that is why he gave a man fourfold mandate that will give you dominion over everything in life (Be fruitful, multiply, subdue the earth control it) Genesis: 1:28 KJV). This is not a prayer request but a command.

The level of your success in life is determined by your understanding of these mandates. Sadly we judge our lives by the condition of the government or situation in our environment, but the truth is that where ever you find yourself is the place of opportunity for you. Instead of people to ask of life what they desire, they rather complain about what already exists around them without making any effort to adjust to them. The problem is as a result of your mindset. When you change, things and people around you will change. When you change the way you look at things, the things you look at will change the way they look. Instead of one to wait only and hoping that things will change, it is better you step out and be the change you want to see. For a husband or a wife that is waiting for the partner to change, stop the waiting and lead the change by adjusting to the way you react to such situations arise, you will see with time those things will fall into place in positive manner.

"The way you think affects the way you are and the results you see".

The secret to life is in your thinking

The content of your thought determines the quality of your life. Remember, you cannot control the thoughts that come into your mind, but you can control the thoughts that you dwell on. You can also develop the type of thought that will dominate your thinking. This can come from what you read or what you listen or watch. This is why the Bible said that we should continually renew our mind with the word of God. When you regularly study the word of God which is an embodiment of wisdom, it will impact your life with the wise thought that will, in turn, influence your decision making and finally affect your pocket. If your pocket is lying to you, it means that you have not told the truth about yourself. Your limitations are whatever you set up for yourself or the ones you allow people to set up for you. This means that you can stand in your way of success. You can be the stumbling block of your life because there are no limitations in this life except the one you perceive. Don't be confused. The truth is that what you see as a restriction, another person might see it as an opportunity.

When the government is bad, a lot of people see it as a limitation to success, but others may see it as an opportunity to succeed. I have heard of people who achieved their biggest goal of buying a facility for their business during the recession when others are selling all they have to sustain themselves. Others are buying those properties at a cheaper rate, and as soon as things change, these individuals will turn to make millions out of those properties. Everything depends on your ability to seize an opportunity for your life.

"Thought is enhanced by rational, analyzed or profitable reasoning. Thought is enhanced by the investment of time into thinking."

Focus leads to actualization

Whatever you focus on, your brain attracts because your brain is designed to direct your life to what you want. When you want to trace the direction of your life, you can bend down to connect with self by counting down your thoughts from what you listen to when you wake up, what you see and what you say or do. When you can account for these three steps, you can trace the direction of your life. For instance, when children are allowed to watch several horror movies, these things are registered in their minds, and it may manifest at a certain period of their lives. That is why it is essential to watch what your children listen to or the games they play because some horror graphics in their games are often wired into their minds and play out after a while. It might be in one, two, ten or twenty years. Whenever the opportunity that is consistent with action comes, it will play out. For some parents who enjoy insulting their spouse before their children or those that hit their wives in front of their children, just understand that you are planting the seed in them and it will grow. Some others like to mock other people. The disadvantages are not just of the children who watched you and have that lifestyle impacted in their brain. It will also shape your life because the content of your thought determines the quality of your life. When you exchange your opinion due to your experience of others, your system will focus on that kind of attributes, and when your brain focus on this negative quality of a person, you will realize that you will always identify this negativity whenever it happens, whether far or near. For instant when you buy a particular clothe with a particular color you will find yourself identifying these colors from all over the places. It is also applicable to a car, you will always identify this type of car all over the place and in some cases you might think that this kind of automobile is common in that location. The truth is that particular vehicle has been in existence but until your brain focuses on it, then it becomes very apparent to you. So when you always identify about specific negative attributes of your spouse, what happens is that your brain is identifying such attribute in you which is evident in another. Similarly, when you get angry over and over on a particular issue, your brain often agrees with that and always point it out to anybody around you in other to keep you in such condition because your mind believed that it is what you want. Your mind does not know when you are choosing a particular lifestyle for yourself and the one you want for another person.

What you feed your eyes your mind retain

Whatever you focus on, your brain will always bring it to you because your brain is designed to do you good by working with you. This is why the Bible says that you should not allow the sun to go down upon your anger Ephesians 4:26 (KJV). What happens is that when you sleep with anger, your subconscious mind never goes asleep. Therefore, it will help to bring about the circumstances that will keep you in that mood because it believes that is what you want. The same thing applies to negativity. When an individual is very negative; such odds will be identified in everything because the brain focuses on such condition. This person can argue with you for a whole year, and they will always see the reason, why such event is negative because that is clouded in their mind. The Bible said to the pure all things are pure and to the impure all things are impure

(TITUS, 1 VS 15 KJV). The same thing applies to people who often see positive in everything. No matter how much you want them to see that things are wrong, they will always see why it is not as bad as you think. Gossip for example, before you gossip, you first hold the negative thought in your mind about someone and then you speak to another person. Your subconscious mind does not know it was for another person and not for you. This is why Jesus asked you to forgive seventy times seven (MATHEW 18 VS 22 KJV) that way you don't hold any negative feeling in your mind. This helps to clarify that forgiveness is not about the other person is all about you. Some of the diseases people experience is as a result of what you wired into your body through your mind. As a result, you may instantly release into your body a stress hormone responsible for autoimmune disorder anxiety or disease. What you hold in your mind always form your reality.

When thought changes, action changes, and
when action changes, outcome changes

The strategy of the enemy to keep you in bondage.

The devil knows this principle, and that is why he deceived people through negative imagination, fear of the unknown, and fear of your health.

- He makes you believe that you will have cancer since your father died of cancer.
- Since your mother had diabetics, you must have diabetics
- Since nobody makes it to university that way you will not make it to university

Whatever you believe comes to you. Job said what he greatly feared has come upon him (JOB 3 VS 25 KJV) and he literarily attracts what he believed. Even though studies show that the genetic traits can be passed down to their offspring but it is not often the case with everyone. That trait might be present, but life is always placed in a balance like a simple pendulum, the side with increase weight will always succumb. So when you focus on such negative, your brain goes after it, and you create the opportunity for the condition to dominate. A lady out of fear declared I would not have cancer like my mother, but she did that in fear and ended up attracting it to herself. But during her treatments, she realizes that she was not strong in the positive but fear, but when she focuses more on the fact that some people battle with such condition and come out alive, she was able to overpower the spirit of that disease and was healed.

"it is possible to live well and live long
if the right principles are applied."

Sometimes the enemy makes you believe someone else is after your life. This may lead you to play safe and thereby attracting what you feared. In some cases, it will play out in your dream as a nightmare in other to create a mental picture that is consistent with such emotion or believe. Therefore, when next you have a nightmare, when you wake up speak the opposite of the experience if it is unfavorable. You need to take charge of your life and stop blaming your family members your parents your country, the president or your neighbor for your misfortune but take charge of your life. I am not saying that parents cannot contribute to your problems but make a conscious decision not to stay in it. The country might be unfavorable to many but to some very conducive. Make a decision that you will function in the circle of those been favored and that way nature will attract all you need to be successful. This is why the Bible emphasized on faith as the substance of things not seen, but evidence of things hope for (HEBREWS 11 VS 1). Without faith, it is impossible to please God (HEBREWS 11 VS 6 KJV) because whoever comes to him must believe in his ability and you will get rewarded for that. When you don't trust yourself how do you think faith in God that you cannot see is possible. If God said, you are blessed and highly favored it means you are already blessed and not going to be blessed. But it will not work for you until you are convinced that you are blessed. It doesn't matter the condition you find yourself or the level of political change that exist around you or in the country. If you have faith in God, you will agree with me that even though you work through the valley of the shadow of death, you shall not fear any evil because the way of escape is already made available by the creator of the universe.

There are no God made failures

As a child, I found myself in what you will consider unfavorable condition, but for me, it was a direction to destiny. It was nature preparing me ahead of time. Buying and selling things to save money for school support since we are many at home and mama and papa were not able to provide enough for us all. This situation of birth looks like a limitation because my life was associated with sufferings. But with strong determination, I identified what I needed from life and focused my choices towards that burning desire. After my first laboratory research in the university, I made a decision to trade the paths of research to understand how diseases develop, how they spread and how they can be treated. With no clue on how to get into such field in Nigeria, I told myself that I would study in the United States to accomplish this desire. When you focus on your dream, it is no longer your job to determine how to bring it to pass just continue with what is available to you while working towards what you don't have. In my case, the business that I started as a child not because I choose to but that was what was available to me at that time. This early in life trading thought me how to do business without vacillation. Apart from giving me the platform to travel to the United States, to become a doctor, it also gave me a heads up to business such that I consider myself a successful international business person and whatever business I set my hand on is already successful. Another person may think my early experience as a limitation, but for me, it is a platform for success. This is why I said nature never makes a mistake. Start operating where you are right now. Stop waiting for things to change before you can be effective. If you like baking, then bake well, if you are selling water package it well and sell. Whatever makes you happy and productive is what will throw you off-balance do it whole hearty. Secondly, whatever you are hoping to get before you can be happy may keep you in misery and unhappy life if such desire is not mate. So be happy were you are and with what you have and work your way till you see other desires manifested.

"Your life is not focused until you have found out what you want out of life."

Chapter Three

YOU ARE UNSTOPABLE

Despite your location, you have been equipped for this battle. First I want you to understand that nature never makes a mistake. This means that wherever you find yourself; this is where you ought to start your function. Whether you are a man or woman, born in the United States or Nigeria, It doesn't matter because you have been equipped by the creator of the universe to do great things despite your gender. When you work with what is available to you presently, you will be able to reach out to the once already existing in the unknown. You have to do this authentically.

One time during graduation I said to myself that

I would research on how diseases occur and will travel to the United States, even though I have no one in the USA. For people around me, it was a foolish talk, but a man with a dream is like a mad man. When they speak it's either termed braggadocios or a worthless talk but with determination and persistence, actualizing the dream is as easy as breathing air. One of my instructor mentioned that "Not until your desire to succeed is as important to you as breathing, your accomplishment is farfetched". When you identify what you want from life, it is your duty to ask for it in prayer, and after praying, you don't seat back doing nothing. There are strategies to receiving your desire. The first is to identify specifically what you want, why you want it and the required actions to accomplish the desired results.

The mistake is that people pray without the corresponding action required to actualize the desire. A lot of people have formed the habit of praying without expecting a result. Others have a list of prayer request to the point that they ask so many things and may not even identify what they asked for when they receive it. In some cases, they may say that it is not the will of God, but the bible said, if you accept Christ as your lord and savior then you are now living in Christ and Christ in you, your will is synchronized with Christ and every request from Jesus is always honored by his father. So the problem is not asking the will of God, but being aware of your identity and who you are in Christ.

"Until a man keeps a vision in front, of him, he will exist in an unusual dimension of time wastage.

All you require to be successful is already in you. Hence, with prayer and conscious strategic actions, you can always change your life for better. The mechanism is in your mind. Stop looking for a solution to your challenges outside you. Use your intuition and focus less on the outside stimulus. Do you not know that you have been well equipped by the creator of the universe? When you understand that everything you need is in you, you will live a fulfilled life. When you ask in a confused manner, your life will be filled with confusion. Some people blow hot and cold simultaneously and this is very unstable. For these individuals, their lives will be very inconsistent. It is imperative for one to understand that your mind always does what you want it to do. It is through what you say or the pictures this is created in your mind. When you change the pictures in your mind, it will change everything. Whatever you believe about yourself is who you are and who you become. As a man thinks in his heart so is he. If you believe that you are limitless, then you will be limitless. If you think you are a failure yes you are, and if you think you are successful, yes you are. Your mind doesn't care what you tell it, and it will attract whatever you tell it.

Use what is in your hand

One time after graduation, I could not get a job, believing that I have no limitation, I prayed and believed that good things are coming my way. However, my life did not change only by praying. I also learned to do something while believing for God's blessings and with 10,000 Naira (Less than $20), I was able to start up a business that changed my life for good. Today I am not seating down waiting for a miracle to happen rather I used what was available to create the miracle that I needed. Do what you can do right. Don't wait for the government to change the dollar rate before you can change your life. When you change your view of life, your life will change for better. In this way, you will not accept rejection. But consider rejection as a platform for success because he who rejects you does not have the capacity to contain what you are carrying. It is essential to always believe that you are well equipped because if you don't, people will use their inferiority complex to destroy your life and destiny. When you are authentic, the energy in your environment will make things work out for you, but you must work inside out.

Believe in yourself

Always declare to yourself, I am sufficient, and I will always be enough. I am beautiful, and the way I am is suitable, I am enough. What you perceive as limitation might be an added advantage. For instance majority of women in the world, today are poor, uneducated, marginalized, terrorized, criticized, miss-gorged, mismanaged, characterized and tolerated.

"A rugged determination to do
whatever it takes to be excellent in
life is the route to the top."

As a woman, there is no need to feel uncomfortable because you had no opportunity to choose your gender before maternal conception and childbirth. The Bible said even when I was in my mother's womb God already knew me and had pre-destined me. So what people think about you does not count but what is important is what you think about yourself. The good news is that your life cannot be determined by what somebody thinks about you. Rather you are shaped by what you think about yourself. As for me, I believe that I am fearfully and wonderfully made by the creator of the universe. When this believes takes root in your life, then you will find the courage to live out your true nature. When you diligently work without complaint and in love, the universe will attract all you need to be successful.

Work inside out.

Working from the inside makes life a lot easier because it allows you to connect with yourself. With the conscious decision, you can change your life. Operating through your authentic self is possible using intuitive energy. When you devote time to identifying yourself, life becomes very easy. Therefore, you have to connect with yourself to make a different because you are unique in nature. Your Intuition helps direct your choices through the real you. Operating effortlessly will assist in creating the right energy because the energy you give is what you get. Depending on your actual self to create the right atmosphere around you. This energy helps you to utilize your natural endowment. Honestly, life success is found within you, and there is no need for people to attribute their inability to have money and other material things to people around and family background. Rather hold yourself accountable for any condition that you are experiencing right now. That is why you can focus on working from within. For instance, a person who often falls into wrong or abusive relationships, instead of waiting for that pattern to continue to re-occur or praying for Mr. Right, that individual need to ask questions concerning her emotions.

What kind of energy does he/she give to people around? Because the energy you give is the energy you get. If you are such a person with a strong bitterness of heart or hard to please, how then would you expect life to change? You will always have set backs because those emotions or habits that drive people away will continuously make you fail in every aspect of relationships. It doesn't matter if you are acquainted with the rich or poor, young or old, educated or illiterate. The problem is not those people but you. Man is the architect of his problems. But identifying that you are the problem and working consciously to avert such problem is the only winning strategy to become successful in relationships.

"It doesn't matter how people acts towards you" what matters is what you are conscious of who you are".

Chapter Four

GOD HAS A PLAN FOR YOU

Your identity is not hidden from the devil. People often say what you don't know don't know you. No matter how much good this sounds, it is inconsistent with reality. Others stated that they had done everything good, but nothing seems to change for the better, and this time, they begin to question what they believed. The reality is that who you are or who you will become is not hidden from the enemy. There is a star for an individual. What I mean is that as soon as a child is conceived, that child already has a star which showcases his identity. A recent scientific article shows that "as soon as a child is conceived (egg is fertilized) there is an immediate spark of light." For those with a great destiny, their star shines differently or brighter than others. This was evident when Jesus was born. The Bible said that three men from the east travelled from far to worship the child. These kings called the magi were not Christians, and they are not from Israel. Despite the fact that the birth of Jesus was prophesied 400 years before he was born, these men, however, did not come to honor God rather they saw a unique identity in a star, and they came.

It is important to note that these men came from different countries. Therefore it does not matter where you were born. It can be in a manger, in the white house or Aso-rock, the location doesn't matter, but the destiny is visible to everyone who understands stars. So the enemy who knows your identity immediately will realize that you are a threat to his kingdom and will position people to help distract you from Gods original plan for your life. For Jesus, he tried first with Herod to eliminate him as a child (Mathew 2 NLT). When he could not succeed, he came with his deception to question Jesus if He was aware or sure of his identity (Matthew 4 NLT). Meanwhile, the bible mentioned that as John the Baptist baptized Jesus, a voice spoke that "this is my beloved son in whom I am well pleased" (Matthew 3 vs 17 KJV). The spirit led him to the wilderness and after his fasting, the deceiver who did not succeed with his target to destroy his destiny as a child through Herod showed up with several twists of the reality of the scriptures. The first thing he questioned was his identity; 'If you are the Son of God, turn the stone into bread". Listen, he did not say are you the son of God, rather he said 'if' you are the son of God. What question is the devil asking you today concerning your identity and destiny?

"Your spiritual root determines
your destiny reach.

One time temptation is not the end

The devil knows how to disguise to be more efficient. In the Garden of Eden, He came as a serpent. Sometimes he can function through a person just as Jesus told Peter to get behind him. He can also come as Judas, your close friends. So do not be deceived the enemy can function as an angel of light. His sole purpose is to steal your joy, to kill and to destroy. In the case of Joseph, the enemy operated through his siblings by promoting them to sell him into slavery. When this same enemy saw that Joseph was not destroyed, he also came through Portiphar's wife to try to lure him into adultery. Who knows what the outcome of that relationship would have been? When the devil did not succeed the second time, he landed him in prison. As for people who whine and question God in unpleasant situations, what can you say in the case of Joseph? The only crime he committed was to be born with a great destiny. After communicating with his family about the dream, he became a threat, and because of jealousy, they hated him and began to plan evil on how to eliminate him (Genesis 39

NLT). The problem is not the particular person to be used by the devil; one needs to understand that the devil is out there to destroy people with a great destiny. Anybody who makes himself available will be used. This individual that might be chosen by the enemy will have some connection with you in other to be effective. This reminds us to take God's work seriously so that he will direct our paths and give us wisdom to fight the enemy.

I mentioned in the first chapter that " <u>You are smarter than the devil"</u>.

How you can withstand the wiles of the devil is to function in the power of the Holy Ghost. The devil who tries to act smart will always map out a strategy to keep you in bondage, but little does he understand that God is the Alpha and the Omega, the beginning and the end, meaning that he knows the end from the beginning. The good news is that the script of your life is already written and each day each chapter is opened and played out. The Bible said even before you were born, I already knew you and had a future for you. There are no God made failures. For to whom He called He predestined. So the strategies of the devil cannot alter the plan of God it, can only delay the manifestation of his desires for your life. When the enemy could not stop Jesus, he decided to kill him but little did he know that it was all part of the plan for Jesus to die. He used Judas, a close friend to accomplish his plan; this tells you that anyone who is available could be used, it doesn't matter how close you are with the person. The same is applicable with Joseph; his blood brothers were used. Cain killed his brother Abel due to jealousy; Peninah was a co-wife of Hannah who chose to frustrate her life. Saul seeks to destroy David; Samson was betrayed by his lover Delilah. It means that anyone who yield himself to the devil, could be used to destroy others but be sure that the enemy will dump you at the end.

Facing the giant of life

When you are trying to rise from one level in life to another, you have the territorial stronghold in that level to fight with. The challenges of life are like a test and the more you write and win the more you will continue to excel in life. No one I know has been able to move from one class to the next level when they failed the exam rather they will continue to rewrite the exam until they pass. My dear arise, arm yourself and fight the good fight.

Chapter Five

WHO YOU ARE

Your anointing is not hidden from the enemy The enemy knows you and what you carry inside you. That is why the man who tried to cast out the demon in Acts of the Apostles received a nasty slap from the demon. When he declared: "Jesus I know, Paul I know and who do you, think you are?" (Acts, 19:15 NLT). Similarly, the guy that was recorded in the book of Mark (5: 2 NLT), this man was found dwelling among the tomb, day and night he was at the mountain crying and cutting himself with stone. But when he saw Jesus from afar, the man ran to Jesus, and the demons cried out with a loud voice and said "what have I to do with you Jesus, Son of the highest God"

(Luke, 8:28; Mark, 5:7&Mthew, 8:29 NLT). With these biblical examples, do you still think the devil don't know you or what is inside of you. I tell you he knows, and that is why he is fighting you. For Jesus, he tried to stop them with a storm to prevent this demonic man from receiving his deliverance.

Do you know how many people the enemy has beaten down today just to ensure that the anointing in them will not come out to save other people? The enemy can perceive your anointing even when you are still in your mother's womb. When he could not succeed, she will plan to take you out as a child. This is why the enemy will use someone to go to schools and shoot innocent children. Do you think that those children have done anything wrong to the gunman? It is because of the seed of greatness in most of this little one that may end up exposing the enemy, and he will try to cut them off at the early stage. This is what happened to Jesus after his birth the enemy sought to cut his life through Herod in other to prevent the world from receiving the gift of redemption that was to come through Jesus Christ

Similarly, after the birth of Moses, trouble

started and the enemy sort to destroy his life through the decree of Pharaoh. One might question how they knew. As a human, we have some intuition either from our dreams or a messenger of God. Once the enemy perceives that, he will throw a combat at you because you are a threat to him. The book of Exodus (1 verse 15 NLT) mentioned that Pharaoh demanded that the whole male child should be killed just as Herod destroyed innocent children after the birth of Jesus. You know what; God the creator who is smarter than his creature often makes a way of escape in such situations. In the case of Jesus, the angels appeared to Joseph in the dream and told him to run with the little child, and his mother to Egypt and they took off in the middle of the night to escape.

For Moses, his mother smartly devised a means to put the little one in a basket and placed him by the river to protect his life. Friends, I am here to tell you that the enemies that have set out to destroy your life have lost out. The reason is that God has made a way of escape for you to safety. The only thing left is that he requires some action on your part. Had it been that Joseph and Mary had not run out, that night before the soldiers arrived early in the morning they might have destroyed the child. That is why I said initially that God is never too soon, or too late he is always on time. Secondly, if Moses' mother did not take action by putting the child in the basket by the river, the soldiers would have destroyed the child who was to deliver the whole Israel from bondage after 400 years.

Think about it my friend, if Jesus did not rise and calm the storm, they might have drowned, thereby hindered from going further and the man on the other side will continue to live in the tomb cutting himself. In other words the challenge in your life is the path way to of greatness. God will always make a way of safety available for you, halleluiah. Your part is to activate the miraculous by your word and action. Not until you act in your part, there is no assurance for safety; you just have to do something to activate the covenant of protection and defense in your life.

The hand of God is on it

Don't worry about the situation as long as you have tapped into the resurrection power. The situation you are confronting might be too bad, and you don't see how you can come out of it, I tell you that same situation is what God will use to elevate you and glorify his name. Certain situation may show up because of God's plan in the future. Consider about the widow who lost his two sons but latter made up her mind to go back to her country where she and her family ran away from due to famine. When she was thinking how she will change her name from Naomi to Mara which means sorrow, God was thinking how to bring forth his son Jesus to save humanity through her daughter- in- law. Does it mean that the famine that drove this family off to Moab in search of a better life was all God's plan to bring forth his son Jesus Christ? One thing is sure that in every situation God is able to turn devils worst to his best.

The Bible said that when Naomi was ready to live the land of Moab, she asked her two daughters-in-laws to go to their father's house since their husbands are late. Orpah kissed the mother-in-law and said goodbye and left. Ruth said no ma'am', please don't ask me to go back because I have a great destiny to catch up. Looking at Ruth a young lady who loved her husband so much and married him and after his death, decided to stay to help the mother-in-law. As a young woman it was devastating to lose her but you know with god that was not the end of the game, rather god was ready to turn the pain and mourning into dancing with Ruth co-operation (Ruth 1-2 NLT). Naomi allowed Ruth to return with her until she was positioned to be the great-grandmother of Jesus. Our god is unsearchable who can allow a problem but bless you with a solution that will blow your mind.

One day I was praying and meditating on God's word when he asks me if there is anything he can't do, even in the midst of the turbulent situation, I answered no because the bible said He can do all things. Yes he said, I can do all things even in the midst of the difficult situations. In another occasion when the storm arose while they were sailing to the other side, He woke up and said "peace be still". The Lord can allow a problem to start because he knows how to receive glory from a turbulent situation. The Lord said to me I can allow a problem but give you a solution to such problem to make your name famous and to bless you. He took me to the book of Daniel and I read how Nebuchadnezzar had a very troubling dream, and none of his sorceress were able to interpret it until God gave the answer to Daniel that result to his promotion (Daniel 2 vs 1 KJV). The same thing happened to Joseph when Pharaoh had a dream, and Joseph was given answer and solution to the situation which led to his promotion as a prime minister. Do you know if you have the solution to all these dreadful sickness or solution to national financial stability, you will become a celebrity overnight? If only you will trust and obey, God is able to use whatever you are going through to elevate you because He never runs out of strategies. He can use anything to bring your blessing even in the midst of difficulties, sickness, helplessness, poverty even in the worst cases of life. Do remember in the bible that it was recorded that Jesus used saliva and sand to restore sight, this has no scientific prove (John 9 vs 6). He moved Joseph from prison to palace, David from Bush to the throne, Hannah from barrenness to fruitfulness, the Shunamite woman from lack to oil distributor, Sarah from barrenness to mother of a great nation. Mary from unknown teenager to be the mother of our Savior, Moses from runaway slave to deliverer, Lazarus from dead to life. Is anything too hard for God to do?

Do not underestimate God because of your scientific proves. He created you and the science. His ways are not our ways. A day is like a thousand years and vice versa. Before God what took you one year to accomplish can take God a day, He said one plus one is one. Again a man shall leave his mother and his father and cling to his wife, and they will become one, one will chase a thousand and two will chase ten thousand, can you do the mathematics? That thing does not make sense does not mean that God cannot make it happen. God is spirit and since the spirit controls the physical, our God is always in control. The generation requires realities and not a bunch of theories and a man with extraordinary thinking will be on top. Everyone is endowed with the power to think and act extraordinarily. Saint Paul said "that I might know the power that raised Jesus from the dead" (Philippian 3 vs 10 NLT). This power makes an ordinary man a champion!

Stop blaming others for your problems

Give up all justification for not being successful. Give up excuses and work towards success. You need to control your thoughts, images, and actions. Remember our mind have an influence on physical matter. Because everything in a word has the vibration of energy and our thought also have vibrations of energy that is very creative. And thoughts can travel 250,000 miles, meaning that thoughts, as well as words have no limit of distance and can be creative anywhere it is directed. Studies have shown that words can transform the molecules of water, just like what we witnessed in the marriage at Canaan (Jn. 2: 1-3 NLT). Since our body is made up of more than 75% of water it means that our thoughts and word have the ability to change water for good or bad. The same way, the thoughts and words you speak about yourself often change the molecular structures of your life. We are wired for love and the bible said that God is love and we were created in the image of God meaning that we are like God. So it simply means that we are love. Therefore, when you operate in hate, rage, anger, unforgiveness, envy and strife, your life is channeled in the opposite direction. When you work in any of these attributes of the enemy, you automatically change the molecular structures of your life. When you work in love, you radiate a positive energy that can change lives. Stay positive at all time for it is essential for healthy and result oriented living. Even though there are several s in this life to make you feel bad, but you have to make a conscious decision to be happy. Whatever you want to have in other to be happy is the thing that the enemy will fight you with. If you are not careful you become the enemy of your life. When you are always attracted to negative people, your subconscious mind will attract such people. My advice is to make sure you know who you are and what you allow into your life. Find something good to be grateful about and be connected to men who encourages you and your positive dreams. As for me, I admire my dentition in the mirror, I do go to the mirror and smile because of the arrangement, and I will say to myself that it was wonderfully made. I will dance around sometimes, and I will go to the mirror and tell myself I am not tall and I am not short, it means I am perfect. I will also say I am not fat and not slim I am perfect. I will say I am not very light skin and not very dark skin, but I am perfect. I was not born the first or the last because I am perfect. When I do this, inside me I am always happy. When I was pregnant and had so many challenges because my husband was not around I felt bad, and to cry. What I did was to scream out loud and then go straight to the mirror while I was still crying and when I looked at the shape of my face. I said to myself that I am not beautiful when crying and started laughing to look good and immediately my mood improved. This is why I say that you need to take charge of your emotion. Change your thought and view about life and everything about you will change.

Your responsibility is to set a goal that is very clear, but it is not your responsibility to determine how to accomplish the target. Once you project the right thing, the solution will come to you. Anything you are attracted to, you have a projection that flows out from you. The energy emitting from you works with your intuitive power; that will land you into the biggest desire of yourself. Do you not know that every of your experiences come to you as a result of fear, thoughts, behavior, what you watch on TV and what you hear all the times, and what you often talk about. That is why it is essential to stay away from negative people or those who complain regularly because when you allow their negative complaints to overwhelm you, your mind will begin to dwell on those things and in a little time you will start to attract such negative energy. One time, a friend, told me how her husband had to spend time with this young man who is always negative and verbally abusive and her husband often complained about him for a long time. One day she realized that he had become too sensitive over minor issues. She was wondering why this sudden changes and she came to understand that the life of his friend imprinted in him and he was influenced by this young man's attitude. The worst part is that what he will be complaining about will always come around and he will complain over and over about it. This happened for a while until she started telling him that this was as a result of his association with this young man.

Whatever you have intense feelings about, you

create into existence. This might be good or bad. Sometimes when things happen, we wish it never happens to us, but fear can attract it to us. Similarly, when you wish yourself some sweet things that you see on the television, you will create such things into existence. It is important to focus on the good parts and not on the bad. When you consciously fantasize about something and talk about it, you will bring it into yourself. But make sure you are always feeling good. Bad mood never brings anything good to you.

Stop complaining

Criticizing people is the worst way to live your life because it is seen as gossiping. So, stop complaining and start living. Look for what you will be grateful for. Gratitude is a key to a successful life. Do things that always make you happy. Do what you are obligated to do but what you feel happy when doing. Do it more and more, be happy and expect something good to happen to you. When you do what you like, all the time money flows, you will make a lot of money when you do what you love; Stop living your life in fear of tomorrow but focus your mind on the right things about yourself.

Chapter Six

ENERGY IN MOTION

Everything in the universe is energy. The human body and the environment according to quantum physics are energy. This means that we are vibrational beings. Don't get it twisted; everything you can see or touch is not just solid. Just as you can see a wall or a house they are all energy and are in motion. Looking at any parts of the human body, for instance, it actually looked solid but according to quantum mechanics, when this part of human body is placed under a microscope, you will see a massive energy emitting from such part of the body. In other words, everything you see is constantly in motion and can change from one state to another. Take for instance the universe contains the galaxy, the planet, the individual and inside human contains organs, system, cells, molecules, atoms, and energy. All these operate in different levels.

When you understand that your life is controlled by the energy around you, then you will work consciously to alter the trajectory of your life and also influence the type of energy you will allow to exist around you. We live in an ocean of motion. The level of vibration that exists in a particular object determines how their existence appears to you. This is because your physical senses translate or interpret the reality of things. So operating by the factors of your sense, you will live your life in a half truth. Because your five senses that control your perception of taste, touch, smell or hearing are controlled by the brain and any malfunctions of the brain will give inaccurate meaning. Since we are vibrations of energy and frequency generators, therefore, working with our physical senses is deceptive because every thought has a frequency that can penetrate anything. That is why the bible said that we do not go by what we see because anything you see is temporal. The perception of how things exist around you is only a matter of your senses, and when you perceive such situation as bad, you will live your life in difficulties. Some other persons might function in the same environment but see things differently, this time in a positive way and will live a fulfilled life.

Have you wondered why two people in the same company, will work with the same level of stress, receive the same salary and the other will live a more fulfilled and happy life than the other? This is a matter of their perception of the environment. In Atlanta, when I started working in banquet services, I used to hear my co-workers complain so much about the nature of the job and some will tell you how miserable they feel. For me, it was a great opportunity to a better life, and all I saw was new opportunities. In this company, once it was time to receive the guest, I feel excited because I knew I would be meeting new people with great opportunities. Instead of been frustrated, I felt joy. Sometimes, my co-workers will ask me if I do get angry at all. How can I be mad at something I see very precious? I am working with all these precious people, and some left me with tips, cards or some wonderful comments on a daily basis.

Therefore, my physical senses are not picking anything negative rather everything in a positive way, but for some of my co-workers they perceive something negative that brings negative impacts and affects their feelings about the job. This simply means that our thought can impact our emotion that controls our life. Whatever you focus on a consistently will be attracted to you both positive and negative. This strategy is not just about thinking positive alone rather it is essential to understand that everything in the universe is interchangeable through the energy generated or energy emitted. Energy frequency scale shows that people that operate in higher energy like love with the frequency scale of 500, joy with scale of 540, peace scale are 600 and enlightenment with 600, have the ability to change their life and those around them.

When your flow of energy works within these high frequencies, it means you can positively impact your environment. When you operate in higher frequency of energy people around you can actually feel it and can connect with you as an individual because it is tangible. Similarly, when you operate on the lower scale of frustrating energy, you can also negatively impact the world around you. This is why it is important to pay attention to who you hang around because they can impact your life positively or negatively. Laughter is contagious; joy is contagious, and the energy around you determines the experience of your life. Even so, what you listen to or what you surround yourself with often impacts your life and that is why you need to constantly renew your mind with the word of God. The Bible said, as you constantly renew your mind with the word of God, like beholding in the mirror you are constantly transformed from one level of glory to another.

Man can restructure their life through the energy of spoken words

The human body is made up of high percentage of water therefore; any emotion that can change the molecules of water can as well impact the body (Dr. Imoto). For instance, a research showed that after speaking to a small quantity of water, this water was refrigerated. When the water was placed under the microscope, the structures of the water with negative words were hideously shaped while the one that were spoken good words to have very beautiful structures. The question is if common statements like I hate you or you make me sick can alter the structure of the experimental water in an awful way, how often have we spoken such words to our body and the body of our children and those around us. Since human body is made up of more than 75% of water and the abnormality in the structure or constituents of the body often create disharmony and when the body is not in harmony, the body will be in disease and the presence of a disease in a body could result to death. This does not often appear in an instant rather such disharmony in the body often alters the structure of the body and can cause any form of disease that may continue to progress until the body deteriorates or result to death.

Take 100% responsibility for your life

Human intension can significantly influence properties, materials, and human realities. Do you know sometimes we are already in communication with some person even before we meet them? Have you wondered why sometimes just immediately after talking or thinking about a person and suddenly the person show up or calls you? This is because man is a spirit being that operate through the mind whereby the physical and nature are controlled. This means that before you physically meet with a person, several communications have taken place in this spiritual realm and the manifestations are witnessed after a while. This is the simple example that we all can relate to at this point. What about the others that happens without us paying attention or identifying with them and how they can impact our lives. Understanding this mechanism will help you to identify how diseases occur. The stress from your brain can be transferred to other parts of the body and create a manifestation or a reaction. The brain has a certain capacity to hold on to nervous energy. Most brain stress are channeled into the organs and heart which may result to chest pain, ulceration, back pain, neck pain, headache, and heart problems due to the adrenaline generated during the stress.

This stress can also be channeled into the heart to cause coagulation of platelets or blood clothing, abnormal heart rate, spasm of the arteries and many more complications that mostly can cause inflammations due to abnormal chemical reactions in the body. This is not a voodoo or juju rather it is a human infliction of problem by themselves that is why I said that you should take 100% responsibility of your life. Several medical conditions are self-environment inflicted. But the irony of this is that due to the level of evil we are attribute to our consciousness of devil in our environment. We tend to attribute most of this self-inflicted problems as demon originated, juju or voodoo manipulation. This is not true what the enemy does is to get people to think that someone is always after them and thereby begin to channel their energy with fear to some kind of warfare prayers that are carried out in fear. One of the vital message in this book is for everyone to understand that whatever you focus on for a long time, you will attract to yourself. So when the enemy pushes you to believe that they have power to inflict certain problems to you, we channel our creative energy into this believe system, thereby creating the physical reality of such problem. I am not saying that the enemy cannot cause things around us, the truth is that several disease of the body is demonic according to the scriptures because when Jesus healed people with different kind of diseases he said, demon of deaf and dumb go, he said demon of infirmity, demons of paralyses go. This means that the demons were involved. But the hidden truth is that God created everything and they are demon free. For example in some parts of the world where their believe system is mostly fetish, people will go to a tree and begin to pour libations on that tree calling different names and enchantment. Since the enemy is working to and fro not having anything to do according to the book of Job. This roaring enemy will now come into that tree or objects and begin to create some activities that such individual will believe. When that person believes that the power is present, without knowing, they give their personal power away to that demon to work with to produce a physical reality. The bible said that all power has been given to Jesus (Matthew 28 vs 18). When Jesus disarmed the devil after his death and resurrection, he took all these powers from him. If the bible said all power was given to Jesus. "All" means everything, so if Jesus has it all so what is it then that is left for the devil. The answer is nothing. Jesus has given us that power, and that power given to us by Jesus is what we give away to the devil. When we believe in his ability to harm us. Just as Adam and Eve gave their personal power away to the devil in the Garden of Eden, the same way, we are individually giving our personal powers away to the devil and he is using it to manipulate us.

Chapter Seven

HAPPINESS IS A CHOICE

Make a conscious decision to be happy. It is your responsibility to make yourself happy not your husband, wife or children. In other words when you chose to be happy, you can actually influence those people around you to also operate with the same vibrations of energy. What I mean is that happiness is a choice. That is why the bible said we should make melody. This will help to change the energy centers of your body. When your energy is channeled in a positive direction, this activates the positive moods that bring about everything that will be consistent with happiness and joy. The same thing is applicable with people emitting negative energy, they attracts negative vibes that is consistent with their mood and they end up attracting things and people that will cause them pain. That is why people say when one thing is bad other things around you become bad. It is not that it just happens from the blue rather when this negative experiences occurs, human mood become very unpleasant and there by continue to emit negative energy that constantly attract such evil. It is not just about the people around you or what they do but it is all about you and what energy is given off by you.

Impact of your emotions and self-reactions

Do you not know that certain emotions and reactions create sickness and infirmity in the body? For example fear, guilt, self-rejection, low self-esteem, self-hatred, self-rejection, anxiety, un-forgiveness, bitterness, pride and rebellion are doorways to sicknesses and disease. When you function within the energy you emit through this reactions, what happens is that doors will be opened for the corresponded infirmity to bash into the body. An emotion of frustration or anger produces an incoherence response in the body in some cases produces some chemical reactions that may result to internal inflammation. This can also trigger certain other diseases such as high blood pressure, sinus and heart attack rooted in fear and anxiety. Diabetics has been associated with self-hatred, rejection and guilt. Certain Cancers is rooted in bitterness of heart, un-forgiveness, slander and resentment. Multiple sclerosis rooted in self-hatred, guilt and rejection from a father. Low self-esteem and lack of love to oneself is attributed to rheumatoid arthritis, or high cholesterol rooted in anger and hostility. Broken spirit and heart break can result to weakened immune system; certain strokes are rooted in self-rejection, bitterness and self-hatred. According to the scriptures from the book of proverb 14 verse 30, envy and jealously has been attributed to bone diseases. Despite that there are witchcraft inflictions of certain diseases but in most cases we are the architect of our problems.

Our minds are like computer and whatever that can impact a computer can as well impact our life. For instance when a virus is introduced to a computer system, that virus will begin to cause malfunction to the system. The same is applicable to human body, when you allow all these emotions to function in you, since they are inconsistent with love, it automatically begin to function as a virus and if the antivirus is not applied immediately, certain files will begin to be corrupted. In human, when those emotions that are devoid of love exists in the body, then certain internal organs, arteries and veins will be impacted even the brain. According to Dir. Caroline Leaf, certain emotion result to making certain choices and those choices can produce certain chemical reactions in the brain that can create problem in the body. When there is disharmony or discordance in the body it will certainly result to Disease if care is not taken.

Your mind is very powerful

Take charge of your mind and determine what happens to you. Disconnect yourself from every attachment that frustrate you and undermine who you are in Christ Jesus. Identify the real enemy which is the devil and not your spouse, your brothers or sisters; fight the enemy not the family members. Be confident and love yourself, don't wish to be like another because you are not as bad as you think after all. Your life is not as bad as you thought and their life is not as good as you thought. Have you taken time to observe the person you want to be like and see the overlaying short comings? May be you are wishing your marriage to be like the other person, and then you need to seat down to observe the other. May be your life may be moving in the right directions than the one you are wishing. It is only in your mind. Just like I mentioned earlier, my facial bone was what I hated most in my body and I always believed that I will have a surgery to remove this cheek bone but as I grew up and mixed up with certain individuals, I realized that they can give high price to have my cheek bone. Someone told me how she had spent money to have it fixed but still not satisfied with the outcome. For me, I received it free from the creator of the universe but due to bully, I thought it was a mistake from God.

The truth is that the bible said that everything made by God is very good. This means that you are uniquely made by the one who created the universe and seed of greatness is already in you. The environment has been equipped to bring such beauty out of you. Remember the bible said that everything was created for him and by him to fulfill Gods desire. Since he already made you into the shape he want you to be, he also made available all that you will need to be successful. But the choice is yours. Remember God cannot force you to choose right but he has made available all that you need. These things cannot be satisfied until you have achieved greatness. Therefore, what you are looking for is looking for you and what you need also needs you. The bible said that money will cry out from the hands that have them. Why because they were all created by God to do good things. However, in the hand of the wicked, it will do evil but in your hand as a good person, it will do great things. So it is important for you to have money in other to do the right things. In all be yourself because all you need is inside of you.

Looking for success outside of you is termed searching without instead of within which is very dangerous. The reason is that you cannot control what other people do but you can control what you do. You may not control the value of dollars but you can consciously use the dollars to get the value of the product you want.

Success is a choice

Success is a choice and everyone makes such decision either in favor or against oneself. This decision to be successful is free when you choose to do something right, then you will be successful but when one make wrong choices that person will end up not been successful in life. If a person also choose not to do anything which is also a choice their life will also follow that direction. Success does not happen at random rather individually you choose to be successful and work towards it. Life doesn't have to happen to you but you can make a decision to make good things happen. This fulfillment of purpose which is called success is connected to knowing and understanding yourself. When you understand who you are, you are already on the ladder of success. Understanding your strength and weakness is a key to fulfillment. As an individual when you understand yourself, and those distinctive capabilities of self, you will use it while managing your weakness. Understand what makes you thick and those things you find pleasure in doing. When you identify what you do without struggling, you find yourself doing it without forcing yourself; such thing wakes you up from the bed. Remember that when you are on the way to success, be ready to encounter opposers or neigh Sayers. These are people who do not believe in your dreams. Do not allow people to talk you out of your desired dream and destiny, rather be focused and determined.

In life, it is essential to answer three important questions; ***who you are?, why you are here and where are you going?*** When you understand who you are and why you are here and where you are going, these will position you on the road to success. Everything begins with understanding self because you are well equipped by the creator of the universe and identifying those things that you have been equipped with, will make you a success. Do not look for this success outside of yourself. Try to have a moment for yourself alone for this is in other words called a moment of self-discovery. Take time for yourself to think about things you do with less effort and people applaud you. This need not be professional activities. It could be something you do at home or among your peer friends. Some people love cooking up stories and tell it like it's true. For such individual, instead of formulating these stories to work against people rather think about formulating this story to improve life which can be effective in the movie industry. Once love is attributed to it in such a way that it favors a person, in that manner you will become a successful person. Do not lavish your plans in a wrong way. Apply that which is in you or what you have been equipped with in a right direction. This is generally adjusting your habit in a positive way to impact your life and that of the people around you in a positive manner.

The environment is not just the problem but you are

The arithmetic's of life is very simple. The problem is not about the environment or the location but the mindset. These things are very simple but men don't believe when it is simple but when you make it look so hard and tedious then men will believe its ability to work. With your right believing you will create in existence that which you desire or you will attract the opportunity to succeed. A problem in the land is not often a bad break for everyone. To some people it is the opportunity of a life time. The king had a dream that was very disturbing and he threatened to kill all the wise men if they did not interpret the dream. For all the other wise men in Babylon, they were all treading on a dangerous ground and on their road to damnation by the kings decree, but for Daniel it was a platform for success since God has a plan to reveal the dream. Being a person of good behavior, it was a blessing in the same circumstance and also for destruction for others. Similarly, the troubling dream of pharaoh moved Joseph from prison to becoming the prime minister in a foreign land. This is why two people in the same business will experience different outcome. One will find himself in a long traffic but focus his mind and attention to listening to his or her most loving music while the other person will be in the same long traffic grawtching, complaining and blaming anyone who contributes to the delay. These two attitudes is just a matter of choice. Therefore, whatever you choose, the universe creates into existence for you.

Chapter Eight

WHAT YOU ASK YOU WILL GET

When a challenge tends to move in a particular direction instead of losing faith try to paint the picture of what you need to understand from that step and when it is clear to you, that place will become your place of turn around. Clear your mind and establish in your mind that nature never makes a mistake; it only gives back the absolute outcome of your choices. When you see your environment as opportunity you will live in harmony with your environment and will have success. The bible said that after Jesus got to Jerusalem on a donkey as a celebrity and appreciated by all, his next discussion with the disciple was that the time for the son of man to be glorified through pain of the cross has come. As a person, it is hard to understand that Jesus will have to endure pain before glorification. In other word, his arrest by the military, the persecution and death were all parts and process of glorification. Therefore, in the midst of your difficulties I want you to see your victory for such is not your last bus stop.

Be in your best behavior and choose to be happy despite what life throws at you. Let the inner happiness and peace in you radiate towards the people around you. The environment will have no choice than to synchronize with you and the universe will attract to you all that is required to maintain happiness in your life. No one is an exception to this truth. It works for both young and old, rich or poor, free or slaves. As long as you put to work an action consistent with the law of the nature, the universe is obligated to respond. Daniel grew up in slavery at the land of patria but he had good behavior and he was singled out in honor. This simply means that where ever you find yourself you can begin anew. Your choices in life will help you function in the right direction. Any city or country you find yourself is the place of opportunity. That is where God have design for your beauty to begin. Do not imagine or hope to be like someone or get to a certain level in other to be happy. Do not always imagine that you can only grow or maximize your potential when you find yourself in another place. This might be delusional because whatever you are looking as your golden desire might be another person's trash but to function within you is the key to success. Some people in Africa believe that they will make it as soon as they travel to the western world. Meanwhile, this person might be doing perfectly well but the thought of greener pastures might lead that individual to sell off all they have and then travel to the western world to end up doing nothing or reduce themselves to menial jobs.

Conclusion

Hope is a powerful force in achieving greatness and living a successful life. With great expectation, life is worth living and happiness is rest assured. The fuel you need to realize your dream is found in anticipating something good to happen with confidence. This force will sustain you even in the most challenging moments. If you are facing a rough time, it is impossible to come to light without hope. In a quest for this sustenance seeking a solution in a wrong part is often detrimental rather connecting to the source of light is the only way to scale higher and God is your endless supply. Finally, you can recreate your experiences for better when you diligently work without complaints and in love, the universe will attract all you need to be successful. Also, life cannot be determined by what someone else thinks about you. Rather you are shaped by what you think about yourself because nature never makes mistakes. Where ever you find yourself that is where you ought to start to function.

Printed in the United States
By Bookmasters